The Brothers KENNEDY

John ★ Robert ★ Edward

Kathleen Krull

ILLUSTRATED BY

Amy June Bates

SIMON & SCHUSTER BOOKS FOR YOUNG READERS
New York   London   Toronto   Sydney

To Rubin Pfeffer
—K. K.

For Peter and Teri, who are wonderful
—A. J. B.

ACKNOWLEDGMENTS

The author thanks Caitlin Krull for getting the ball rolling
and Alexandra Cooper for keeping it in the air.

The illustrator thanks Laurent Linn.

SIMON & SCHUSTER BOOKS FOR YOUNG READERS
An imprint of Simon & Schuster Children's Publishing Division
1230 Avenue of the Americas, New York, New York 10020
Text copyright © 2010 by Kathleen Krull
Illustrations copyright © 2010 by Amy Bates
All rights reserved, including the right of reproduction in whole or in part in any form.
SIMON & SCHUSTER BOOKS FOR YOUNG READERS is a trademark of Simon & Schuster, Inc.
For information about special discounts for bulk purchases, please contact
Simon & Schuster Special Sales at 1-866-506-1949 or business@simonandschuster.com.
The Simon & Schuster Speakers Bureau can bring authors to your live event.
For more information or to book an event, contact the Simon & Schuster Speakers Bureau
at 1-866-248-3049 or visit our website at www.simonspeakers.com.
Book design by Laurent Linn
The text for this book is set in Berkeley Oldstyle.
The illustrations for this book are rendered in watercolor, gouache, and pencil.
Manufactured in the United States of America
1209 PCR
2 4 6 8 10 9 7 5 3 1
Library of Congress Cataloging-in-Publication Data
Krull, Kathleen.
The brothers Kennedy : John, Robert, Edward / Kathleen Krull ; illustrated by Amy June Bates.
p. cm.
ISBN 978-1-4169-9158-8 (hardcover)
1. Kennedy, John F. (John Fitzgerald), 1917–1963—Childhood and youth—Juvenile literature.
2. Kennedy, John F. (John Fitzgerald), 1917–1963—Juvenile literature. 3. Kennedy, Robert F.,
1925–1968—Childhood and youth—Juvenile literature. 4. Kennedy, Robert F., 1925–1968—Juvenile
literature. 5. Kennedy, Edward M. (Edward Moore), 1932–2009—Childhood and youth—Juvenile
literature. 6. Kennedy, Edward M. (Edward Moore), 1932–2009—Juvenile literature. 7. Presidents—
United States—Biography—Juvenile literature. 8. Legislators—United States—Biography—Juvenile
literature. 9. Brothers—United States—Biography—Juvenile literature. 10. United States. Congress.
Senate—Biography—Juvenile literature. 11. Kennedy family—Juvenile literature. I. Bates, Amy June, ill.
II. Title.
E842.Z9.K785 2010
929'.20973—dc22
2009033499

★ ★ ★

"We stand at the edge of a New Frontier . . .

the frontier of unfulfilled hopes and dreams."

—*JOHN*

"We are a great country, a selfless country, and a compassionate country."

—*ROBERT*

"We are all part of the American family, and we have a responsibility

to help members of that family when they are in need."

—*EDWARD*

★ ★ ★

★ J O E ★

John Kennedy lived to tease his tough big brother, Joe. When Joe wasn't looking, John would steal the frosting off Joe's slice of cake. Instantly a fistfight would start, and John would lose. But John never stopped teasing Joe, thinking that one day he'd win. It just wasn't in him to give up hope.

Hope, compassion, and loyalty—these were what mattered to the Kennedys, a prominent Irish-American family in Boston. But to the nine Kennedy children—Joe, John, Rosemary, Kathleen, Eunice, Patricia, Robert, Jean, and Edward—it was also important to *win*.

Joe once told a friend, "You know, I'm the oldest of my family, and I've got to be the example." He was seventeen years older than the youngest, Edward. The older Kennedys inspired the younger ones to do better—at sports, at school, and at the dinner table, where they talked about what they had read in the newspaper that day.

Joe had heard about the NO IRISH NEED APPLY signs in certain parts of Boston. But he was so used to winning that even as a boy he talked about rising to the top and becoming president of the United States. The idea of an Irish Catholic in the White House was unthinkable—except to those who knew Joe.

★ J O H N ★

More than anything, John hoped to prove himself the equal of his idol, Joe. But John was almost constantly sick. Robert would joke, "If a mosquito bit my brother, the mosquito would die."

During John's hospital stays, visitors could hardly see the boy for the stacks of books around him. John was the biggest reader in the family.

On walks around Boston with Robert, John would talk about strong leaders like George Washington, Lawrence of Arabia, and King Arthur and his knights. By reading about these heroes, John came to believe that one person really could change history through deeds of hope, compassion, and loyalty.

Even when they were young, it was clear that the Kennedy brothers were headed for politics. John made his first public speech when he was just six years old, in honor of his grandfather, the governor of Massachusetts.

John never became as good at sports as Joe was. In the evenings John would practice passing the football hundreds of times, until it was too dark to see. Over the years he lost hope of becoming a football star, but gained the hope of becoming a leader. He liked to gather his younger siblings around the fireplace and tell them about leaders in history, those who used their power to make people's lives better.

In high school John ran for freshman class president and lost. But in his senior year he was voted "most likely to succeed."

★ R O B E R T ★

Robert was the quiet one, struggling to keep up with his idols, Joe and John.

At age four Robert decided to teach himself to swim as well as they could. Over and over he'd jump into the icy ocean off Cape Cod.

Over and over his brothers would dive in and rescue him—until he could swim on his own.

Robert was the first to call "That's not fair" whenever he thought others were breaking football rules. He never joined in bullying—so compassionate that he'd even try to stop it when he could. Riding the train to high school, he saw poor neighborhoods from the window and started questioning how America could allow such inequality.

He was so serious that John called him "Black Robert."

★ E D W A R D ★

When the youngest Kennedy was born, fifteen-year-old John asked to be the baby's godfather and suggested the name "George Washington." His parents chose "Edward" instead.

Edward's older brothers taught him how to swim and sail, ride a bike, throw a football, and pillow-fight. Together they protected their sister Rosemary, who developed special needs.

Edward loved to make his brothers laugh and loyally followed them everywhere, even when they jumped off cliffs. "I was pretty scared, but they all seemed to be doing it," he said later.

With each brother putting pressure on the next, Edward got the most. As with his brothers before him, it was important to Edward to win. In both sixth and seventh grades he was elected to class office.

"IN A CRISIS," JOHN ONCE SAID, "FAMILY MEMBERS are the only ones you can count on." The Kennedy children were enormously proud of one another and always defended each other. And no one was prouder of them than their father. He couldn't wait for his children—especially his four sons—to start serving their country. The first big step for both Joe and John was going off to fight in World War II.

Joe, the most promising of the Kennedy sons, never had a chance to run for office. He died at age twenty-nine as a fighter pilot in the war, and the Kennedys never really recovered from the shock of losing him.

That left three brothers—John, Robert, and Edward. Their parents had raised them with the values of hope, compassion, and loyalty, the same values that guided them as they went on to lives of public service.

After the war ended, John started to run for office. The entire family focused on helping him win his first election in 1946. During his fourteen years in Congress, John continued to read about heroes in history and urged his brothers to learn about them too.

Finally, in one of the closest elections ever, John was elected the first Catholic president, our youngest president, a president with a whole new hope for the future. He set out to be the kind of heroic leader he had read about, someone who made people's lives better. Yes, America was a great country, but so much more could be done.

"Ask not what your country can do for you," he said. "Ask what you can do for your country."

John was the first president to speak about equal rights for African Americans, saying that this change would not happen without new laws to end discrimination.

He announced a goal of putting a man on the moon within the following decade.

He started the Peace Corps as a way of bringing hope to the poorest countries in the world, and thousands of Americans volunteered to serve.

He encouraged people, especially young people, to enter public service and be part of something great and hopeful.

Many people started to use him as their role model—a leader and inspiration in his own right.

One thousand days into his presidency, John was shot and killed.

Hundreds of thousands of people came to his funeral, standing in a line three miles long, with millions more crying as they watched it on TV. That a life full of such hope and promise could be cut short at age forty-six was a shock that anyone alive then will never forget.

And then there were two brothers.

Robert had grown up to become John's best friend and main advisor. Though Robert could act tough, he also knew how to put himself in other people's shoes. Even from a young age, he had felt compassion for those living in poverty in America. Now just the thought of it made him sick to his stomach. After John's death Robert's compassion became a fight to get rid of injustice.

As a senator and later a presidential candidate, Robert traveled unpaved back roads in the Mississippi Delta to meet with starving children. He marched with Mexican migrant workers to fight for the rights of those who pick our fruits and vegetables. He visited American Indians on reservations, appalled at the living conditions. Poor people and minorities, groups that felt ignored by politicians, were especially excited about Robert.

But while running for president, Robert was shot and killed.
And then there was one brother.

Edward had grown from being the family clown to being his brothers' most loyal supporter. During their campaigns he could always be counted on, seeming to be everywhere at once. Whenever John was sick and his voice failed, Edward spoke in his place. While stuck in a traffic jam, Edward would jump out and offer campaign bumper stickers to the other drivers.

When Edward became a senator at age thirty, his very first speech was on civil rights for African Americans. It was his way of being loyal to John's memory.

After Robert's death Edward carried on his brother's commitment to compassion, pouring his energy into making laws that protected the most needy people. Lugging a briefcase full of papers home with him every night, he was usually the most prepared person in a meeting.

As a senator for more than forty-six years, Edward worked on laws that helped just about every man, woman, and child in America. He served in the Senate for longer than almost anyone else in its history.

In 2008 Edward's doctors warned him that he was too ill to travel. But back in the 1960s his brother Robert had predicted that a black president would be elected within forty years. Edward was not going to miss seeing Barack Obama accept his presidential nomination.

"For me this is a season of hope," Edward said in his own speech that night. "New hope for a justice and fair prosperity for the many, and not just for the few."

Less than a year later, he died.

Hope, compassion, and loyalty—the brothers Kennedy
inspired these in one another.
And so they have inspired others ever since.

★　★　★

"Let the word go forth from this time and place, to friend and foe alike, that the torch has been passed to a new generation of Americans."

—JOHN

"Each time a man stands up for an ideal, or acts to improve the lot of others, or strikes out against injustice, he sends forth a tiny ripple of hope."

—ROBERT

"I believe that each of us as individuals must not only struggle to make a better world, but to make ourselves better, too."

—EDWARD

(pages 4–5) With his business ventures, the Kennedys' father, Joseph, had become the richest Irish American in the world. Active in politics, he and his wife, Rose, poured tremendous energy into raising their children. All of the kids were expected to be able to sing, tell a story well, recite poetry, and play—both indoor games like charades and outdoor sports like skiing, riding horses, swimming, sailing, tennis, and above all, touch football, for both girls and boys. Magazines published articles about how unique the Kennedy family was.

(pages 6–7) Every night at dinner, each boy was expected to be able to debate current events. Rose pinned up daily newspaper clippings, and the boys had to be prepared to defend their views about that day's Supreme Court decision, or events in Russia and the Middle East, or discrimination against the Italians and the Irish, and especially the latest plans from President Franklin D. Roosevelt to help those suffering from the Great Depression. Asking questions was encouraged, as was disagreeing, as long as one was polite to frequent guests. The guests included prominent foreign visitors, actors and musicians, and politicians like the former mayor of Boston—John F. Fitzgerald, their own grandfather.

(pages 8–9) As an adult John was diagnosed with Addison's disease, a failure of the adrenal glands, about which little was known during his childhood.

Whether he was well or sick, his favorite type of reading was always biography—books about other people. "All history is gossip," he once said. When asked what his best trait was, he would say curiosity.

All the Kennedy brothers experienced instances of anti-Irish prejudices. When John was ten, his father moved the family from Boston to a town just north of Manhattan, in part because he felt discrimination was not going to be as big a problem there.

(pages 10–11) John's ill health continued into high school. He was so skinny that the other boys called him "Rat Face." Being in and out of hospitals increased his sense of compassion for others to whom life dealt blows. The only boy at his school with a subscription to the *New York Times*, John became aware of how the stock-market crash of the Great Depression was hurting ordinary people, and he saw that government had to take the lead in helping. As a junior he wrote an essay called "Justice" that showed his keen awareness of social injustice.

(pages 12–13) Robert felt pressured about holding his own in his brilliant family. He once said, "As the seventh of nine children in a competitive family, I had to keep getting better in every way just to survive."

About Robert's dives into the ocean, John said later, "It showed either a lot of guts, or no sense at all, depending on how you look at it."

(pages 14–15) Robert was the only one of the four brothers who met his father's offer of one thousand dollars if he didn't drink or smoke until age twenty-one.

In 1951, while in law school, Robert invited Dr. Ralph Bunche, a prominent African-American diplomat, to speak to his all-white campus. When other student leaders protested, Robert told them, "You're all gutless!"—and he eventually prevailed.

(pages 16–17) The brothers took care of Rosemary, watching out for her, playing dodgeball with her, making sure she danced at parties. Many believe that dealing with Rosemary's special needs—she was diagnosed as mentally disabled—fostered the other Kennedy children's compassion. Rosemary lived at home until she was twenty-three, when an experimental surgery led to her living in an institution.

(pages 18–19) Robert and Edward, too young to fight in the war, stayed behind, taking walks with their grandfather Fitzgerald to look at the landmarks of their history-rich city. Robert later served in the navy, Edward in the army.

(pages 20–21) As the Kennedy children turned twenty-one, their father presented each with a fund worth over one million dollars. America, land of opportunity and freedom, had been good to him. Now he wanted his sons to serve their country without having to worry about money. Great things were demanded of them. As their mother quoted from the Bible, "Of those to whom much has been given much will be required." And as Robert later remembered, "It is more important to be of service than successful."

The women were to do good deeds as well, but as was the case with women in that era, not in the public eye. The Kennedy sisters worked hard on their brothers' campaigns. In addition, Jean served as ambassador to Ireland from 1993 to 1998, and Patricia founded the National Committee for the Literary Arts at Lincoln Center in 1981. Eunice became an advocate for the developmentally disabled and, in 1968, a founder of the Special Olympics. After Eunice's death in 2009, Edward said, "If the test is what you're doing that's been helpful for humanity, you'd be hard pressed to find another member of the family who's done more."

Only three years after Joe Jr.'s death, Kathleen died in a plane crash at age twenty-eight, another blow to the family—especially John, to whom she was closest.

=====

(pages 22–23) John, as commander of the *PT-109* boat, had emerged as a hero from World War II, rescuing most of his crew after his boat was attacked and sunk in the Solomon Islands in the South Pacific. He was also admired for *Profiles in Courage*, his book about eight senators who risked their careers to speak out about their beliefs.

In his first election John went door-to-door to meet everyone in his district, saying to each, "My name is Jack Kennedy. . . . Will you help me?" He went on to six years as a representative and eight years as a senator.

As a senator John wrote about the "special contribution of the Irish"—their endurance during "centuries in which their mass destruction by poverty, disease, and starvation were ignored by their conquerors."

=====

(pages 24–25) The 1960s were a dramatic time for social change, and John was at the forefront as president, speaking for many. Inspired by Martin Luther King Jr., John made a famous speech introducing his civil rights bill: "All Americans should have the same rights regardless of their race." In 1964, during the following administration of Lyndon B. Johnson, Congress passed the Civil Rights Act, setting the stage for long-overdue equality under the law.

John's goal of putting a man on the moon was reached in 1969, meanwhile spurring a surge of interest in scientific accomplishment.

The Peace Corps is still going strong after almost fifty years, with some two hundred thousand volunteers having served.

With his glamorous wife, Jacqueline, and two charming children, Caroline and John Jr., John presided over a White House that cultivated creative people from all walks of life. Some called his administration "Camelot," after the legendary court of King Arthur, one of John's heroes. The first president to speak directly to the public on a regular basis, John held sixty-four televised press conferences, making many people feel as if they knew him.

=====

(pages 26–27) By asking for so much change, John angered some people and made many enemies. On November 22, 1963, a loner named Lee Harvey Oswald was arrested for shooting him while he rode in a Dallas motorcade. Then, two days later, Oswald was killed by Jack Ruby, the owner of a nightclub in Dallas. Ever since, debate has raged about who was actually behind the assassination.

=====

(pages 28–29) After law school Robert worked as a lawyer investigating corruption. Later he managed John's campaigns, working eighteen-hour days, and served in his presidential cabinet as attorney general.

In a speech on the night Martin Luther King Jr. was killed, Robert said, "What we need in the United States . . . is love, and wisdom, and compassion toward one another."

He was the one who thought that civil rights was the most urgent problem in America and prodded John to act.

Robert became closely identified with children, American Indians, Mexican Americans (working with migrant worker hero Cesar Chavez), and the millions of Americans he thought needed help. He campaigned for president hoping to champion the overlooked, as well as end the Vietnam War, which he thought was a terrible mistake.

=====

(pages 30–31) Robert, too, made numerous enemies. Eighty-five days into his campaign, he was assassinated by Sirhan Sirhan, a Palestinian who hated Robert's support of Israel. Two million people came out for Robert's funeral train, the largest turnout for a nonpresident ever.

=====

(pages 32–33) Robert gave Edward advice as they walked together on Capitol Hill—but also sometimes told him to solve his own problems. (This echoes a day when both boys were in school and older boys were picking on Edward. He saw Robert and called for help. Robert walked on, saying, "You've got to learn to fight your own battles." It was his way to show compassion—he truly thought this would help his baby brother the most.)

After Robert's death many urged Edward to leave public life. But he said, "Like my brothers before me, I pick up a fallen standard. Sustained by the memory of our priceless years together, I shall try to carry forward that special commitment to justice, excellence, and courage that distinguished their lives."

=====

(pages 34–35) Edward became one of the most influential senators ever. His special cause was fighting injustice, whether regarding health care, civil rights, women's rights, immigration, the disabled, the poor, or the elderly. Fellow senators called him "the single most effective member of the Senate" (John McCain) and "the most remarkable senator I've ever worked with" (Joe Biden). Barack Obama called him "an American who has never stopped asking what he could do for his country."

In response to the Hurricane Katrina disaster in 2005, for example, Edward insisted, "We are all part of the American family. When members of that family are in need, in want, and in fear, we all have a duty to make our family whole once more."

Mid-1840s: All four of Joseph Kennedy's grandparents emigrate from Ireland to the United States. They are fleeing the Great Hunger, the famine during which one million people died and another million left Ireland.

1846: Rose Fitzgerald's ancestors begin emigrating from Ireland to the United States.

1914: Joseph Kennedy and Rose Fitzgerald marry and settle in Brookline, Massachusetts.

1915: Joseph Jr. is born.

1917: John is born.

1918: Rosemary is born.

1920: Kathleen is born.

1921: Eunice is born.

1924: Patricia is born.

1925: Robert is born.

1928: Jean is born.

1932: Edward is born.

1940: John graduates from Harvard University and later publishes his senior thesis as a book, *Why England Slept*. Joseph Jr. serves as a delegate to the Democratic National Convention.

1941: Rejected by the army for health reasons, John joins the navy with his father's help.

1944: Joseph Jr. dies in World War II.

1946: Campaigning with his grandfather, the former mayor of Boston, John wins election to the House of Representatives.

1948: Kathleen dies in a plane crash. Robert graduates from Harvard University and enters the University of Virginia Law School.

1952: With Robert managing his campaign, John wins election as a Massachusetts senator.

1953: Robert begins working as a lawyer on various Senate subcommittees.

1954: Edward graduates from Harvard University and enters the University of Virginia Law School.

1956: John hopes to become the vice presidential nominee, on the ticket with Adlai Stevenson, but is edged out.

1957: John's book *Profiles in Courage* wins the Pulitzer Prize for Biography.

1960: Again with Robert managing his campaign, John is elected president of the United States at age forty-three, narrowly defeating Richard Nixon.

1961: John appoints Robert his attorney general to enforce America's laws.

1962: Edward is elected as a Massachusetts senator.

1963: President Kennedy is assassinated in Dallas, Texas.

1964: Robert is elected as a New York senator.

1968: Robert announces his candidacy for the presidency. After winning the California primary later that year, he is assassinated in Los Angeles.

1980: After announcing his candidacy for the presidency, Edward wins primaries in Massachusetts and nine other states, but loses in fourteen states and withdraws his bid.

1995: Patrick Kennedy, one of Edward's three children, becomes the youngest member of Congress as a Rhode Island representative. Kathleen Kennedy Townsend, one of Robert's ten children, becomes lieutenant governor of Maryland.

1999: John F. Kennedy Jr., son of John and editor of a political magazine called *George*, dies in a plane crash.

2006: Edward wins an eighth term as senator.

2008: Edward endorses Barack Obama for the Democratic presidential nomination. Later that year, doctors diagnose Edward with a cancerous brain tumor and he undergoes surgery. John's daughter, Caroline, a lawyer and author, campaigns for the New York Senate—to replace Hillary Clinton, now secretary of state—but later withdraws her name from consideration.

2009: Edward dies at his home in Hyannis Port on Cape Cod, Massachusetts.

Burns, Ken, director. "The Work to Come" (2008 Democratic Convention Tribute to Senator Edward Kennedy). http://www.youtube.com/watch?v=a2r9mQ7bUco.

Canellos, Peter S., ed. *Last Lion: The Fall and Rise of Ted Kennedy*. New York: Simon & Schuster, 2009.

Clarke, Thurston. *The Last Campaign: Robert F. Kennedy and 82 Days That Inspired America*. New York: Henry Holt, 2008.

Clymer, Adam. *Edward M. Kennedy: A Biography*. New York: Willam Morrow, 1999.

Collins, Thomas P., and Louis M. Savary, eds. *A People of Compassion: The Concerns of Edward Kennedy*. New York: Regina Press, 1972.

* Cooper, Ilene. *Jack: The Early Years of John F. Kennedy*. New York: Dutton Children's Books, 2003.

* Harrison, Barbara, and Daniel Terris. *A Ripple of Hope: The Life of Robert F. Kennedy*. New York: Lodestar Books, 1997.

John F. Kennedy Presidential Library & Museum. http://www.jfklibrary.org.

Kennedy, Edward M. *True Compass: A Memoir*. New York: Twelve, 2009.

Kennedy, Maxwell Taylor. *Make Gentle the Life of This World: The Vision of Robert F. Kennedy*. New York: Broadway, 1999.

O'Brien, Michael. *John F. Kennedy: A Biography*. New York: St. Martin's, 2005.

Robert F. Kennedy Center for Justice & Human Rights. http://www.rfkcenter.org.

Salinger, Pierre, Edwin Guthman, Frank Mankiewicz, and John Seigenthaler, eds. *An Honorable Profession: A Tribute to Robert F. Kennedy*. New York: Doubleday, 1968.

* Sommer, Shelley. *John F. Kennedy: His Life and Legacy*. New York: HarperCollins, 2005.

Speak Truth to Power, a division of the Robert F. Kennedy Memorial. http://www.speaktruth.org.

Thomas, Evan. *Robert Kennedy: His Life*. New York: Simon & Schuster, 2000.

(*FOR YOUNG READERS)